FOURTEEN ZEBRA

FOURTEEN ZEBRA

Written by
Henry Carroll

Illustrated by
Nigel Howlett

John Blake

Published by John Blake Publishing Ltd,
3 Bramber Court, 2 Bramber Road,
London W14 9PB, England

www.blake.co.uk

First published in hardback in 2006

ISBN-13: 978 1 84454 285 7
ISBN-10: 1 84454 285 8

British Library Cataloguing-in-Publication Data:

A catalogue record for this book is available from the British Library.

Design by Henry Carroll and Nigel Howlett

Printed in Spain by Bookprint SL

1 3 5 7 9 10 8 6 4 2

Papers used by John Blake Publishing are natural, recyclable products made from
wood grown in sustainable forests. The manufacturing processes conform to the
environmental regulations of the country of origin.

This book is testament to the fact that our current knowledge of the world equates to a mere flea, quietly sucking the blood from the neck of a giant Madagascan sea gorilla.

Prof. Hilary Z Jameson

Flea expert

An Introduction

Disappointed at coming second in a *Reader's Digest* list of the world's greatest geologists, **Henry Carroll** decided to embark on a voyage of discovery in search of the most elusive of all geological trophies: the world's softest diamond. His epic journey took him into the depths of the Pacific Ocean and to the iciest reaches of Siberia. Shortly after receiving news he had slipped a further two places down the list, a freak typhoon left Carroll separated from his guide, and marooned in the jungles of central Africa.

Meanwhile, following a gruesome incident with a defective pole vault, the former athletics sensation, **Nigel Howlett**, turned his hand to drawing. Soon, armed only with a pencil and sketchpad, he departed for the Congo on an open-ended drawing holiday. It was during this time when he first laid eyes on the ancient rock carvings of the Wacca-Dacca tribe. Howlett spent years in the jungle learning how to decode their hieroglyphs, eventually discovering they translated into a map, marking the location of a rare crystal, so soft, you could mould it in your hands.

Two nights later, the hand of fate intervened – lost and delirious, with no food or water, Carroll unexpectedly rode into camp on the shoulders of a giant silverback gorilla named Colin.

Together, they found the diamond but then, in a bizarre tribal ritual, ended up accidentally eating it. With Howlett's new-found love of drawing, and Carroll's semi-competent knowledge of the natural world, the duo soon embarked on a gruelling four-year journey to unearth the most extraordinary facts from around the globe. The results of this will stretch our understanding of the small planet we live on to the very limit.

Welcome to the world of FOURTEEN ZEBRA

The most common cause of death for fish is extreme dehydration.

Every two months, the Royal Mint conducts an official 'wrinkle inspection' of the Queen's face.

Scientists are of the belief that there are three colours in the spectrum yet to be discovered. It is rumoured one of them could be a fourth primary colour and look something like this:

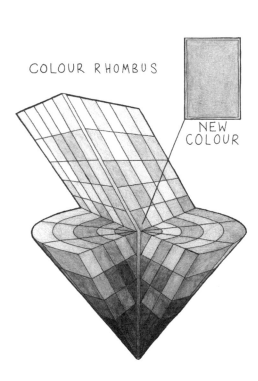

COLOUR RHOMBUS

NEW COLOUR

London Zoo will lose, on average, fifteen chameleons a year.

Unbeknown to their owners, 43 % of household cats
live at two different addresses.

Dogs are the only animals able to eat and sleep simultaneously.

Guy Fawkes endured so many days of torture on the rack, he officially became England's tallest man.

One of the contributing factors as to why the Great Fire of London spread so quickly was a fundamental design flaw in early fire engines, which were made of wood.

Career criminal 'Ricky the Rake' was so skinny he was able to escape from prison three times simply by walking through the gaps between the bars. His unique escape method was foiled on Christmas day 1965, when after eating too much turkey, he became stuck.

23rd November 1998

Never have I experienced cold like this. It has
penetrated me right through to the bone and I can feel
the twinge of frostbite on the end of my nose. I do
not know if Howlett will survive the night. I have
loaned him a blanket made from the finest Siberian
llama wool as well as my penguin skin balaclava, given
to me by an old Inuit friend, Hoshi.
The central heating has broken down and the hotel
porter is nowhere to be seen, even the kitchen is
closed. I can only pray that the six-course dinner we
finished an hour ago will keep us going. Tomorrow,
following a final delivery of typewriter ribbons and
putty rubbers, we set off on our monumental
expedition; will I be leaving alone, or will my
companion survive the night? As always, only time
holds the answers.

The Ritz

The heating in the Ritz is strictly monitored
and we do not take kindly to any unauthori
dismantling of hotel property. I am left wit
choice but to bill you for the cost of re

With compliments

The scientists responsible for cloning 'Dolly the Sheep' sprayed the following markings on both her and the original sheep:

The annual 'Leap of Faith' competition, held in Wales, sees contestants long jump over a line of women called Faith. The world record is currently held by the mountain goat herder Hugh Stevens, who managed to leap over thirteen Faiths.

While making some final adjustments to his
newly crafted execution device, Joseph Ignace
Guillotine inadvertently became the first person
to be executed by it.

FOURTEEN ZEBRA

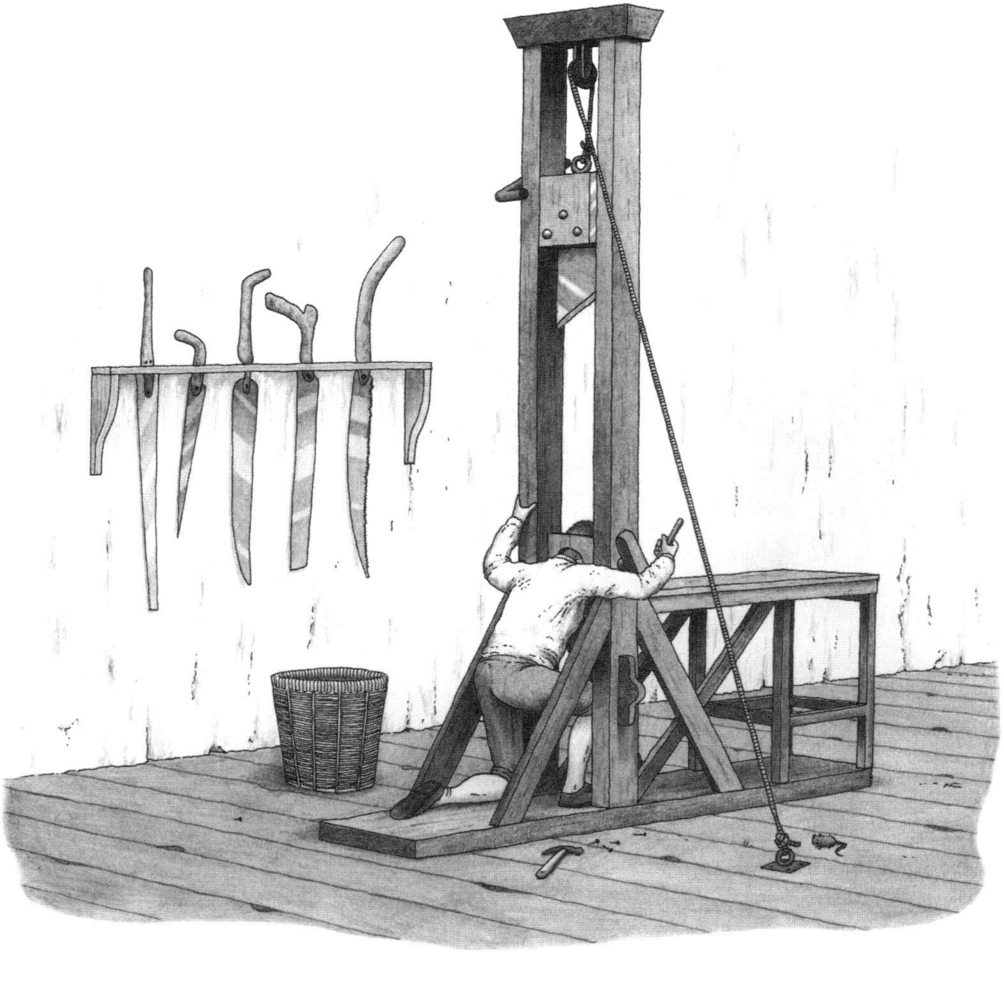

Following the beheadings of Anne Boleyn and
Catherine Howard, Henry VIII had commemorative
postage stamps made depicting their severed heads.

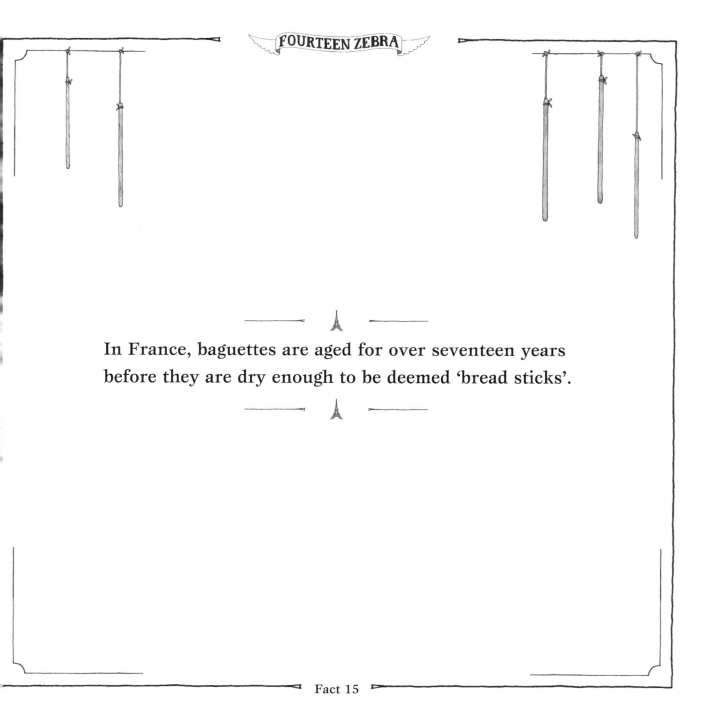

In France, baguettes are aged for over seventeen years before they are dry enough to be deemed 'bread sticks'.

Whilst listening to a nightingale in the Black Forest, the German composer, Gustav Schimberg, claims to have heard the bird sound a new note. Schimberg is in the process of modifying his grand piano in the hope of replicating the sound which he has provisionally called 'H'.

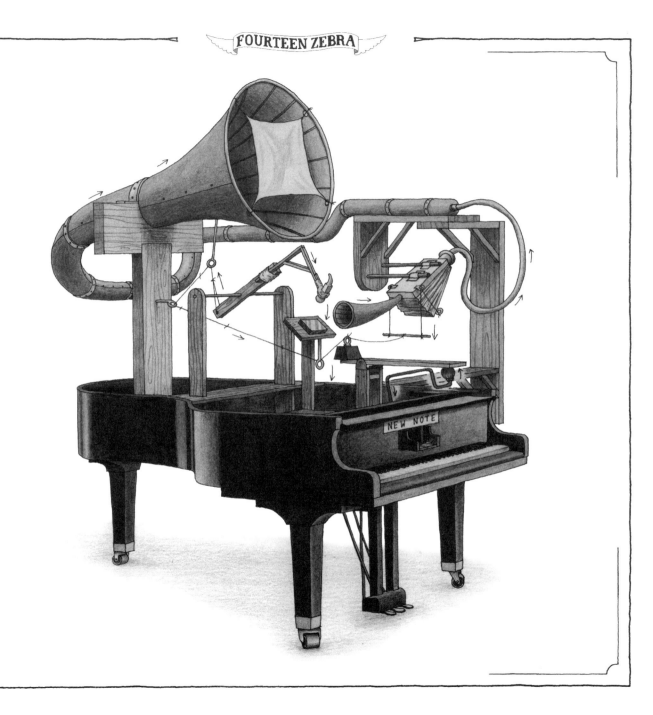

In May 1976, a seven-year-old boy from Minsk was lifted twenty-three feet off the ground whilst holding fifty-seven fully inflated helium balloons.

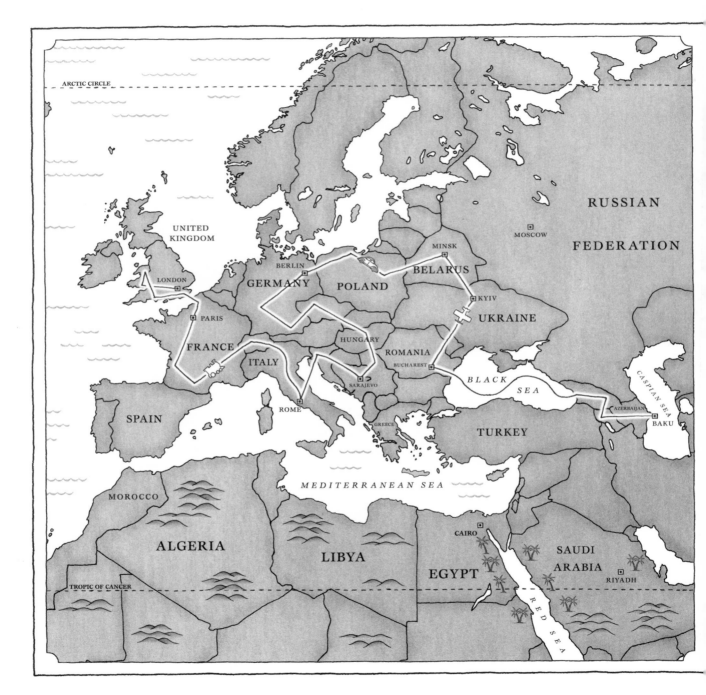

19th March 1999 - Baku

Sometimes we inhale so much dust in the Azerbaijan
State Library we do not feel hungry for lunch.
Overall, the librarians have been very
accommodating and assisted us in finding historical
documents which have not been disturbed for
thousands of years. Unfortunately, last Thursday
Howlett mistook an ancient Dead Sea Scroll for a
roll of lavatory paper - not only did we have our
library cards temporarily revoked, but we also
spent the night in Baku city penitentiary.
Thankfully, I was alone in my cell. However,
Howlett was not so lucky. He has still not spoken
since being released.

The heaviest object ever to be successfully floated in the Dead Sea is a 500kg anvil.

(A feat achieved by Benny Gilmore in 1998)

The most complicated position ever achieved
in a game of Twister is as follows:

The purest form of water is found in the hump of the Arabian camel, *Camelus dromedaries*.

The oldest unbroken world record dates back to 1241BC. It is held by the ancient Egyptian Pharaoh, Ramses II, who escaped from a mummification suit in two minutes and thirty-nine seconds.

If all the boats were taken out of the world's oceans the sea level would drop by two centimetres.

The following data has also been calculated:

Whales and other large sea creatures	3.16*
Shipwrecks	2.19*
Undiscovered bounty	1.75*
Messages in bottles	1.14*
Albatross	0.33*
Icebergs	0.28*
Ray-Bans	0.08*

*All data calculated in 'cm' using measurements taken in June 1998

One of the earliest tools ever invented was a cutting device made using the head of a dried sawfish.

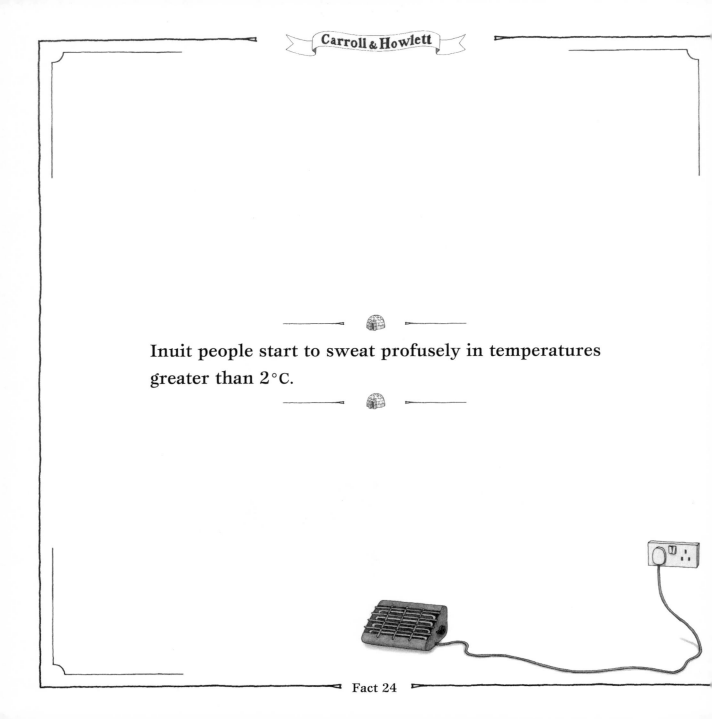

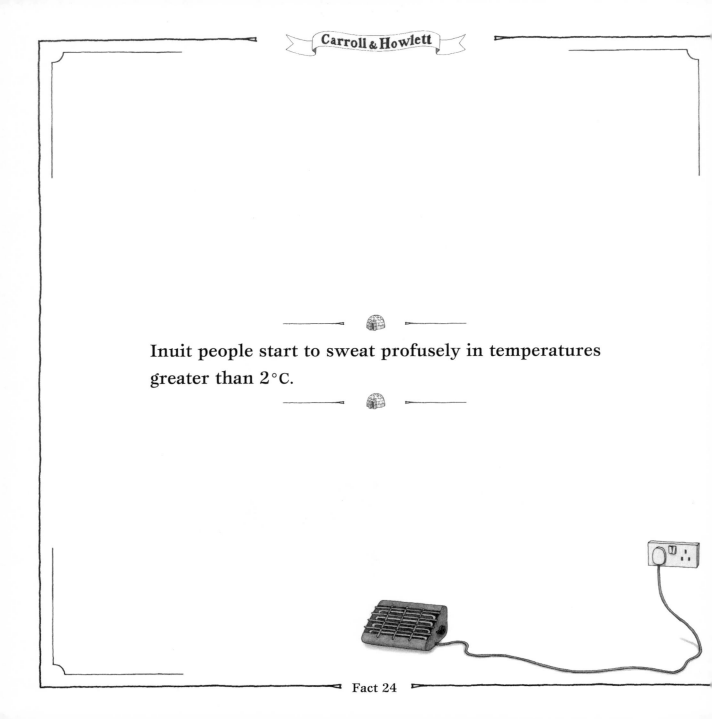

Inuit people start to sweat profusely in temperatures greater than 2°C.

In 1946, during an expedition in ancient Egypt, Dr Wensley Whitaker became separated from his team while searching for the mythical ice urn of King Combi-Jombi. When the rescue team finally found him alone in the desert it transpired the doctor had spent two days and nights dancing and drinking in 'Club Pharaoh', before realising the whole place was a mirage.

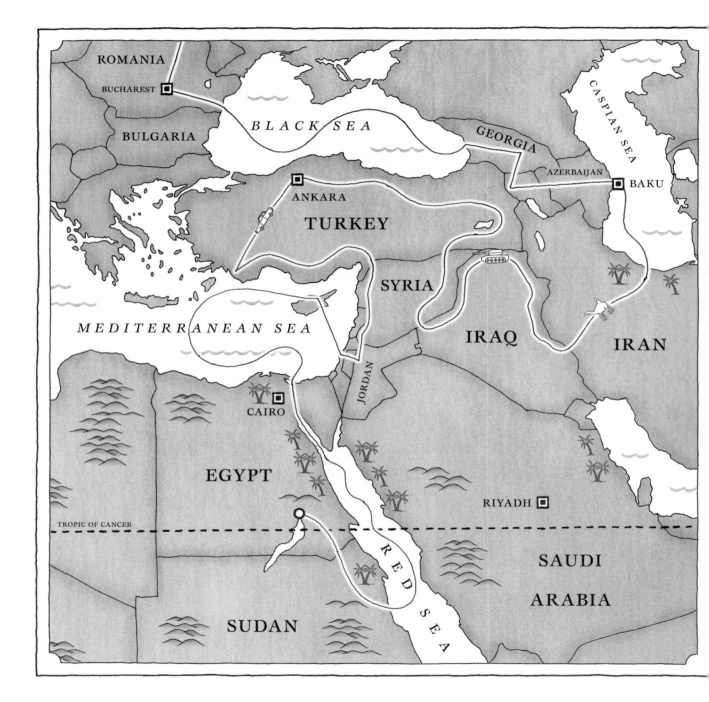

7th June 1999 - Egypt

After arriving at the ancient Egyptian tomb of King
Tutankhamen it was disappointing to discover that all
the gold and jewels had already been plundered,
especially as our seventeenth sponsorship cheque from
the Royal Society of Exploration is now long overdue.
Nevertheless, it is comforting to see that the tomb is
still untouched by the unstoppable blight of mass
tourism and the potent scent of Howard Carter still
lingers in the air.
Regrettably, Howlett has decided to leave the
expedition and go off on his own. I am not sure when
our paths will cross next. Then again, looking at the
timetable, I see his camel ride tour lasts only
forty-five minutes which incidentally leaves every
seven minutes from the main entrance hall and costs
only two Egyptian Pounds.

CAMEL RIDE TOURS

The official camel tour to the tomb of King Tut!

"Amazing! The camels were so comfy!" (Colin Cooper from Reading)

"I was scared at first but Omar was so helpful and his safety demonstration
was very thorough" (Marion Cooper from Reading)

Monday to Friday 9am - Midnight	Saturday to Sunday - 10am - 11pm				
		TIMES		And	2.00pm
TOUR STOP	9.00am	9.07am	9.14am	then	2.03pm
	9.03am	9.10am	9.17am	every	2.10pm
Main Entrance Hall	9.10am	9.17am	9.24am	7 mins	2.30pm
Howard Carter Corner	9.30am	9.37am	9.44am	until	2.35pm
Tomb	9.35am	9.42am	9.49am		2.45pm
Café	9.45am	9.52am	9.59am		
Shop					
Entrance Hall	notice and are subject to camel union guidelines			And	11.00pm

King Tutankhamen
1999
ONE TOUR
Camel Tours!
33210

Amazon women would use their severed
breasts as decorative purses to carry war paint.

Several examples of these are on display at the Macedonian Museum of Feminism.

The man-eating Egyptian tuna is the only fish
to have a fully functioning pair of legs.

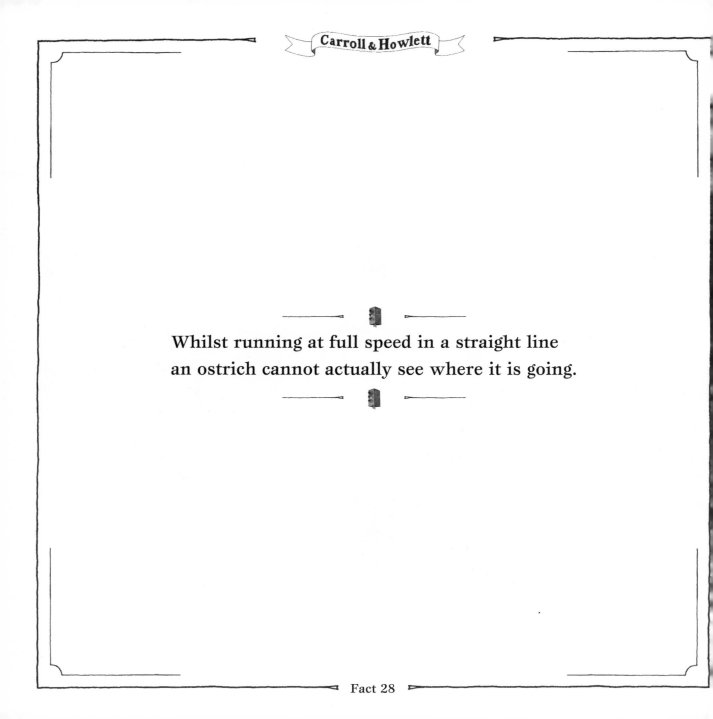

Whilst running at full speed in a straight line
an ostrich cannot actually see where it is going.

The impact of a bird-poo excreted from an altitude in excess of 400ft would kill a man on the ground, instantly.

The only creature to have an odd number of legs
was the large plant-eating dinosaur, Apatosaurus.

Over 86% of the crocodiles which inhabit the
banks of the Ganges are vegetarian.

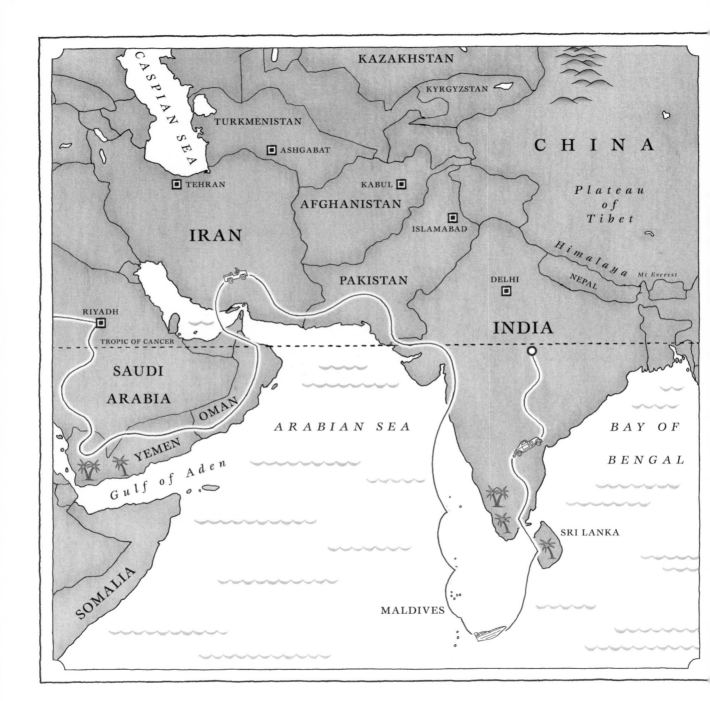

23rd September 1999 - Central India

Tonight we had the honour of receiving a dinner
invitation from the Maharishi and four of his senior
gurus. The dinner was a little too exotic for my
palate. However, I believe Howlett enjoyed the meal as
I noticed him slip an extra sheep's eye into his pocket
for later.

As three of the gurus have not spoken for over
thirty-two years, dinner conversation was, to say the
least, difficult. Moreover, on observing their messy
eating habits, I suspected the others had not fully
come round from a gruelling four-day long
trans-subliminal, existential meditation.

The mood lightened somewhat when Howlett suggested we
play the central Indian game of 'speed scribing' - the
Maharishi is legendary for the speed at which he
scribes, and is able to copy out the entire Yellow
Pages, word for word, in under forty-five minutes. By
the time Howlett had reached 'ABSEILING WINDOW
CLEANERS', the Maharishi had already finished! Luckily,
a nearby guru made an official recording of the time
which it transpired was a new world record -
incredible.

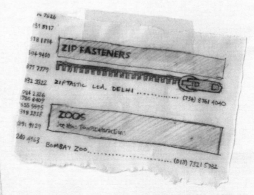

If a mosquito were the same size as modern-day man its needle would be strong enough to chisel through the outer marble walls of the Taj Mahal.

The nomadic tribes who roam the lower mountainous
regions of the Himalayas have 423 different words for air.

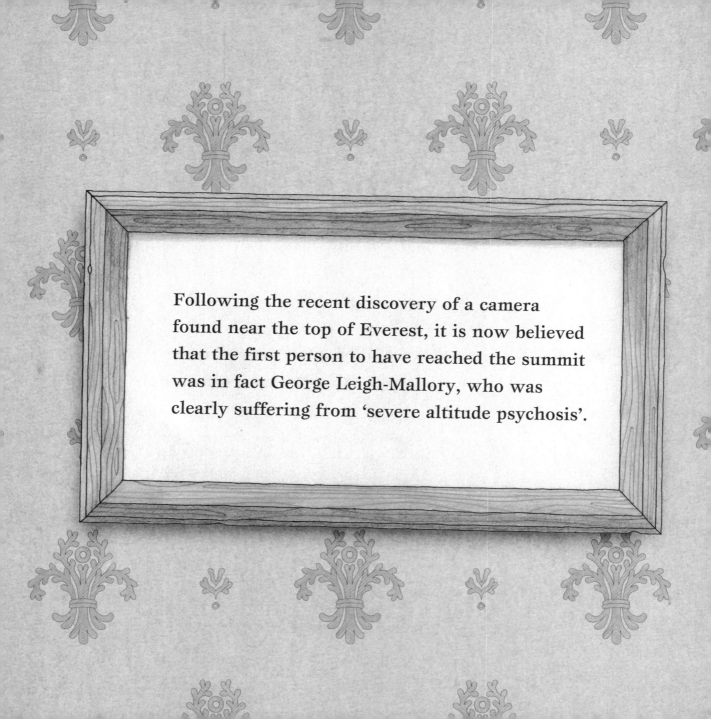

Following the recent discovery of a camera found near the top of Everest, it is now believed that the first person to have reached the summit was in fact George Leigh-Mallory, who was clearly suffering from 'severe altitude psychosis'.

Due to the increase in air pressure, approximately twenty-three Himalayan mountain goats are crushed each year when they unknowingly wander below altitudes of 9000 feet.

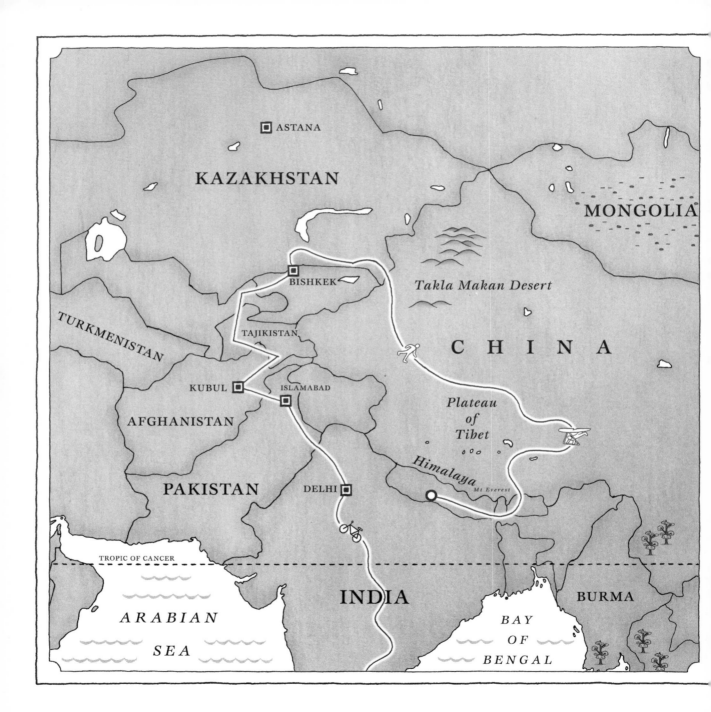

1ST DECEMBER 1999

ONE YEAR INTO THE VOYAGE AND SUPPLIES ARE DANGEROUSLY LOW.
HOWLETT HAS RUN OUT OF ACID FREE CARTRIDGE PAPER AND HIS
TRUSTED 8B IS ALMOST DOWN TO 3CM (I HAVE PLEADED WITH
HIM NOT TO PRESS SO HARD, BUT HE SIMPLY DOES NOT
LISTEN). I HAVE CARRIED OUT SUCCESSFUL NEGOTIATIONS WITH
OUR TIBETAN SHERPAS AND THEY HAVE AGREED TO LET ME TATTOO
NOTES ONTO THEIR CHESTS. FOR EXTRA RATIONS, SOME OF THE
LESS WEATHERWORN HAVE EVEN LET ME USE THEIR FOREHEADS.
IN RETURN, I HAVE PROMISED TO SHIP THEM BACK TO LONDON FOR
TRANSCRIBING.
I MAY HAVE ALSO TOLD THEM OF A LETTER I RECEIVED FROM HER
MAJESTY QUEEN ELIZABETH II, WHICH STATES THAT FOR THEIR
SERVICES TO THE CROWN, THEY WILL EACH BE GIVEN A
'COMMONWEALTH PASSPORT' AND A PART-TIME JOB AT ONE
OF THE MOST EFFICIENT CALL CENTRES IN WINDSOR. MOST
OF THIS IS THE TRUTH.

In 1999, 'Mental Connect Four' became more popular than chess and is now Russia's most played game.

Garry Primakov (pictured here on the left) is the current champion.

A man's testicles are the exact same size and weight as his eyeballs.

Erno Rubik, inventor of the Rubik's Cube,
has never managed to complete his puzzle.

The second tallest creature on the planet is the
long-legged Siberian llama which has limbs
over two and a half metres long.

The densest cloud ever recorded was a cumulonimbus above the Russian city of Novosibirsk. The late meteorologist, Herbert Schumacher (1935-2000), was so confident of the cloud's density, he climbed out of a helicopter and stood on it for a total of 4.2 seconds.

A team of trackers once tagged an ant in the Gobi Desert and then followed it for over 1,600 miles to Canton, south China. The ant averaged a speed of just under 2mph.

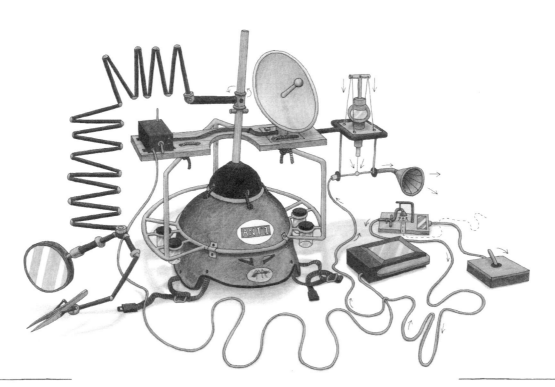

ARCTIC CIRCLE

Central Siberian Plateau

S i b e r i a

RUSSIAN FEDERATION

Lake Baikal

□ NOVOSIBIRSK

KAZAKHSTAN

MONGOLIA

ULAN BATOR

Gobi Desert

KYRGYZSTAN

Takla Makan Desert

BEIJING □

NORTH KOREA

SOUTH KOREA

C H I N A

YELLOW SEA

Himalaya

INDIA

EAST CHINA SEA

5th May 2000 - The Gobi Desert

With our funding substantially reduced, compromises
have had to be made with expenditure. Teaming up with
a BBC camera crew seemed like a good idea at the time
but unfortunately relations have already become
strained. They are filming a new documentary about the
elusive three-humped Mongolian camel which I have
assured the producer does not exist. Yet he adamantly
disagreed and showed me an article he had read in
Camel Monthly magazine. To settle the argument, he
challenged me to five rounds of knuckle-dusters.
However, after only the second round our hands began
to look swollen, and we agreed to disagree.

6th May 2000

Petrol stations are a basic affair on the eastern
fringes of Outer Mongolia, and I was disappointed at
the team's reaction when I thoughtlessly lit a
cigarette whilst refuelling their equipment truck.
Although we no longer have any cameras, Howlett has
kindly agreed to sketch any camels we come across, and
seems confident that he can make a broadcast quality
flick-book.

The most calming yoga position is the 'Pretzel of Peace'.

At any one moment, there are approximately seven people in the world stranded on desert islands.

The highest number ever spoken aloud is reported to be 780,801,041,091,273,557.

The world's smallest grain of sand was found by Shane Bishop on a beach in New South Wales, Australia.

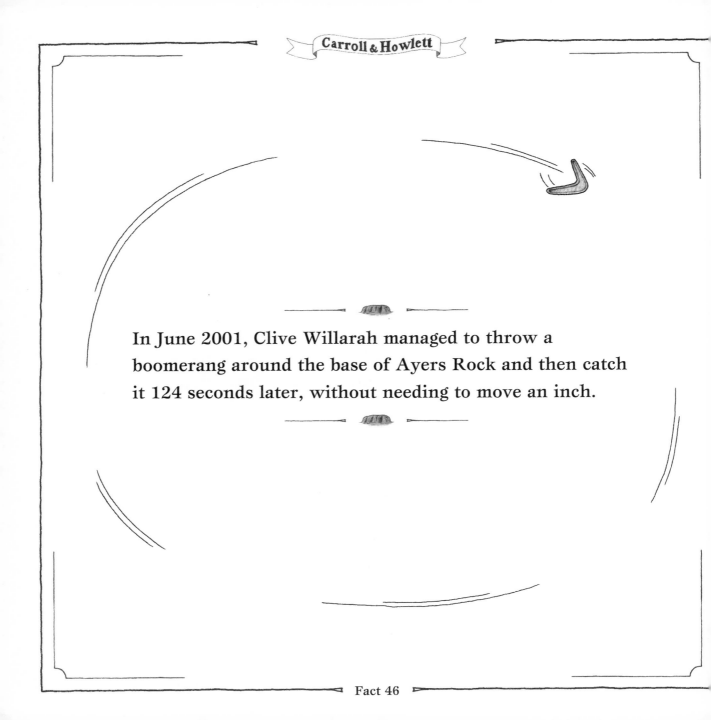

In June 2001, Clive Willarah managed to throw a boomerang around the base of Ayers Rock and then catch it 124 seconds later, without needing to move an inch.

Australians living on the underside of the planet are three times more likely to suffer from random spells of dizziness and passing out.

The late meteorologist and eminent cloud expert Herbert Schumacher is the only person to have ever recorded a perfectly cuboid cloud.

When in the mother's pouch, a joey will only
manage around three hours of sleep per week.

The urine of the Australian desert husky is so concentrated it can dissolve sand.

Before 1923 pilots refused to fly through clouds
as they were feared to be too solid.

The random ordering of letters on eye-test charts
was only introduced in 1959 after opticians became
suspicious about a sudden rise in the number of
people with apparent 20:20 vision.

42

During his lifetime Douglas Adams signed so
many copies of his books that the ones containing
no signature have become more valuable.

42

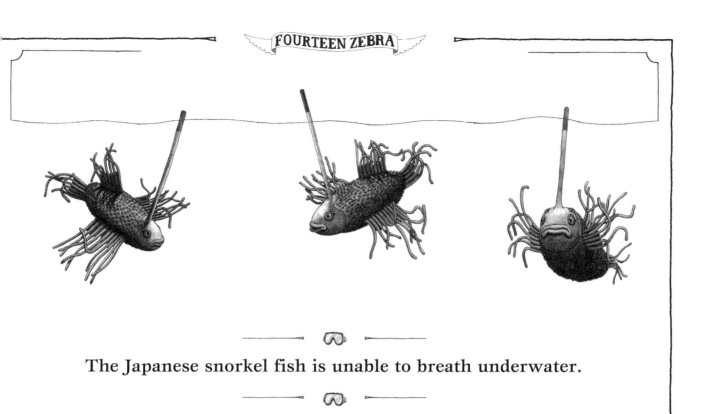

The Japanese snorkel fish is unable to breath underwater.

By the year 2028 mobile phone technology will be so advanced that users will only require tiny implants in their hands; the little finger will have a small mouthpiece and the thumb a microscopic earpiece.

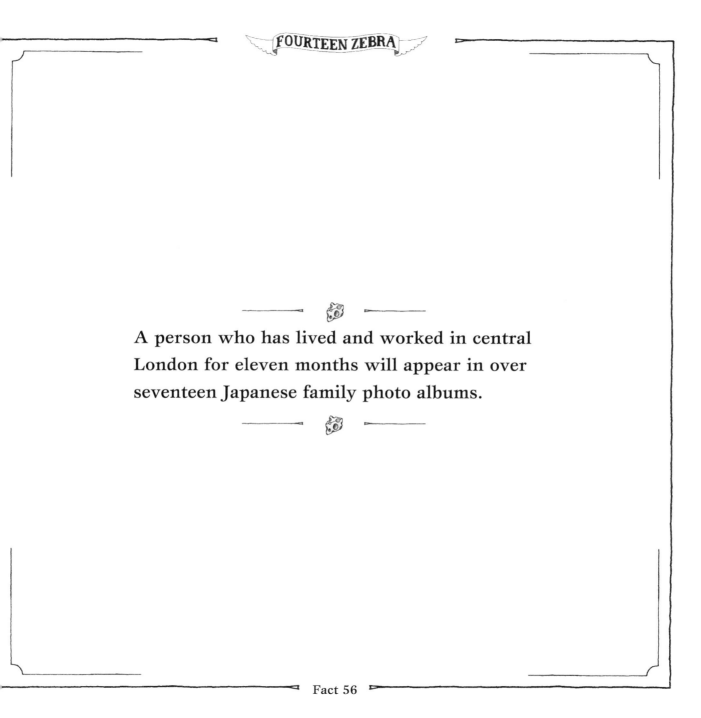

A person who has lived and worked in central London for eleven months will appear in over seventeen Japanese family photo albums.

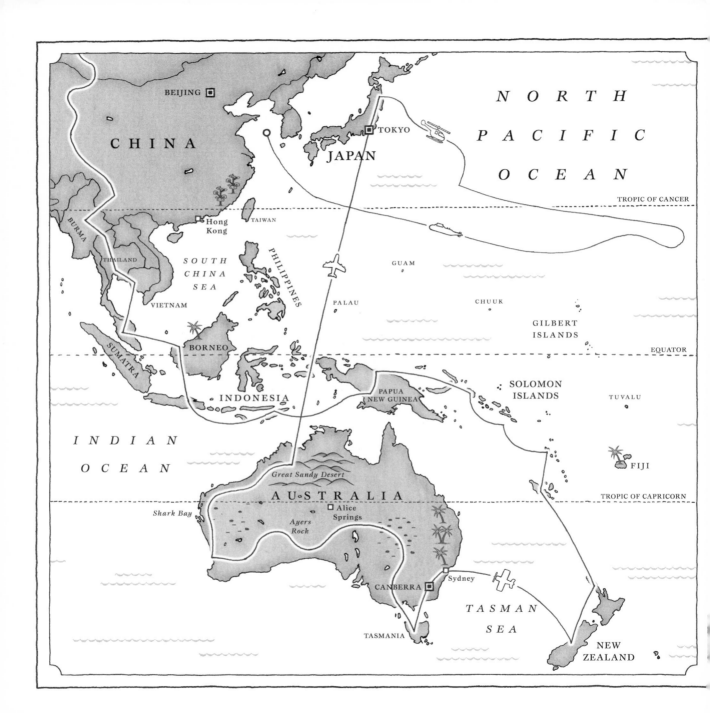

NORTH

PACIFIC

OCEAN

TROPIC OF CANCER

CHINA

BEIJING

TOKYO

JAPAN

Hong
Kong

TAIWAN

BURMA

THAILAND

SOUTH
CHINA
SEA

PHILIPPINES

GUAM

CHUUK

VIETNAM

PALAU

GILBERT
ISLANDS

EQUATOR

SUMATRA

BORNEO

INDONESIA

PAPUA
NEW GUINEA

SOLOMON
ISLANDS

TUVALU

INDIAN

OCEAN

FIJI

Great Sandy Desert

AUSTRALIA

TROPIC OF CAPRICORN

Shark Bay

Alice
Springs

Ayers
Rock

CANBERRA

Sydney

TASMAN

SEA

TASMANIA

NEW
ZEALAND

ROYAL
NAVY

12th January 2001 - somewhere below the surface of the
Yellow Sea

It is much easier than one might expect to accidentally
fire off a cruise missile while aboard a nuclear submarine.
However, Admiral Sandecker's quick thinking and cool head
meant that before long, the missile would self-destruct
somewhere in the clouds above Tokyo.
We are aboard Intrepid, the newest addition to the Royal
Navy's fleet which is kindly transporting us across the
Pacific.
Howlett has done a sterling job at integrating himself
with his new environment, and the crew seemed more than
happy to show him the inside of the reactor chamber. As
far as I know, he is still in there, sketching the core.
The Admiral has expressed much interest in our expedition
and was especially keen to see our documentation of a
North Korean air force base which we inadvertently drove
through while on route to Seoul. After faxing the notes to
the Prime Minister, we have been ordered to change course,
and lay low in the Yellow Sea.

It could now be sometime before we reach El Salvador.

In 1957, the American Navy blew-up the Japanese island of Yokkatocca as continental drift was causing the landmass to advance rapidly into US waters. Yokkatocca would have reached San Francisco Bay in the year 2001.

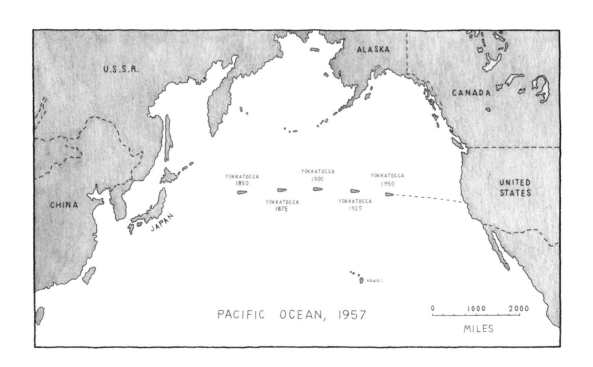

The only recorded occasion when an iceberg has floated
up the river Thames was in January 1803.

Each year an average of three Inuit children are eaten whilst attempting to cuddle polar bears.

Tests conducted during the winter months of 2001 confirmed that the bang needed to wake a hibernating grizzly bear must exceed three hundred and fifty decibels.

The Pentagon employs over fifty insect trainers
dedicated to teaching cockroaches the correct
protocol to follow in the event of a nuclear war.

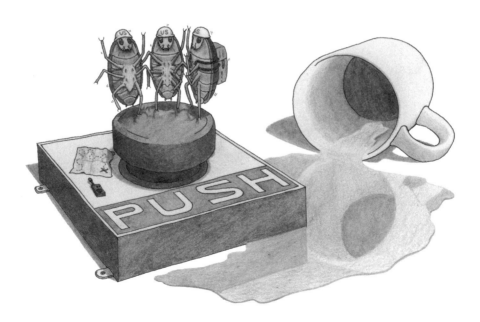

The late Bill Connors, a fifty-eight-year-old sales manager from Michigan, was discovered to be dead at his desk after being left undisturbed for fifteen days. It was only noticed that Bill had passed away when the office cleaning lady asked him to lift his legs so she could sweep under his desk.

When the world's largest geyser erupted on June 3rd 1972, the tourist Frank Caffery inadvertently snapped the following iconic photograph:

Frank & Barbara

Barbara at Old Faithful
Honeymoon, 1972

Contrary to popular belief, in the early 1990's
the most photographed woman in the world was
not Princess Diana but Clare Bryant, the security
guard who stands at the main entrance to the
Houses of Parliament.

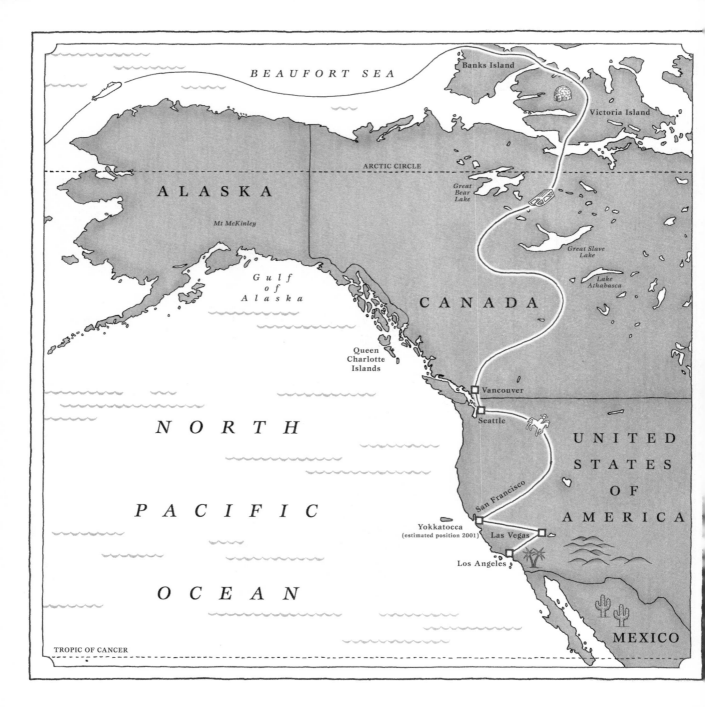

14th April 2001 — the Hollywood Hills

We only agreed to star in this Hollywood film on the
proviso that a personal chef would be on hand at all
times and we are not woken before 10am. At least we
have separate trailers and a chauffeur driven golf
buggy. However, after taking some careful measurements,
I am most concerned that Howlett's trailer seems to be
fifteen square feet larger than mine. Apparently, it is
because he has a speaking part and I only play a mute
photocopy repairman. Nevertheless, this still does not
explain why he gets an entourage of make-up girls and
follicle hygienists. He must need it more than I!
I am still not entirely sure what this film is about.
The director assures me that it is an 'art-house'
feature, and will mostly be improvised. To make matters
worse, Howlett is having trouble remembering his only
line, which, I have to say, is not that complicated. It
reads, "I'm not sure if your typing skills are good
enough to be my secretary Stacy (long pause) is there
anything else you might be good at…?"

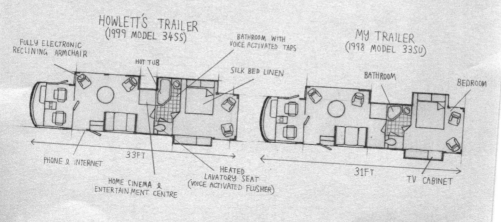

HOWLETT'S TRAILER
(1999 MODEL 34SS)

FULLY ELECTRONIC
RECLINING ARMCHAIR

HOT TUB

BATHROOM WITH
VOICE ACTIVATED TAPS

SILK BED LINEN

MY TRAILER
(1998 MODEL 33SU)

BATHROOM

BEDROOM

PHONE & INTERNET

33FT

HOME CINEMA &
ENTERTAINMENT CENTRE

HEATED
LAVATORY SEAT
(VOICE ACTIVATED FLUSHER)

31FT

TV CABINET

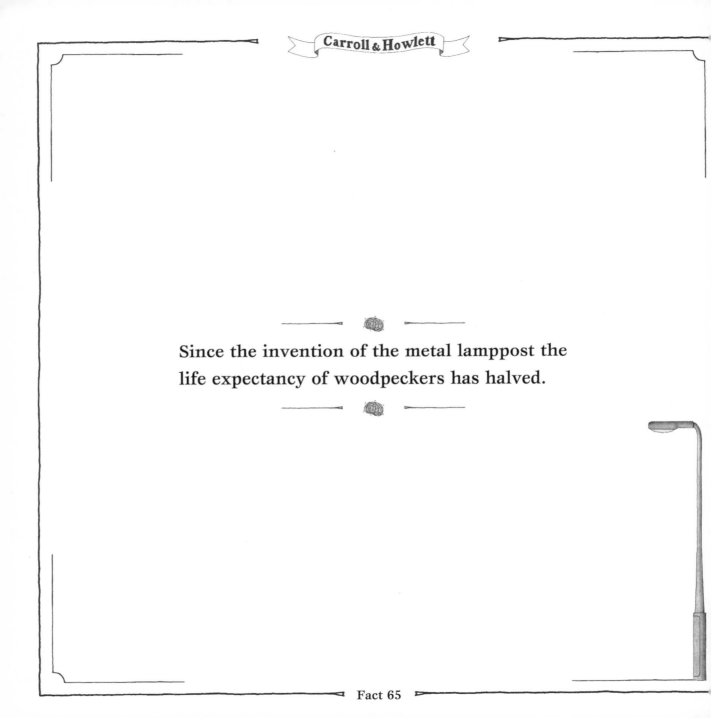

Since the invention of the metal lamppost the
life expectancy of woodpeckers has halved.

It is predicted that by the year 2052 the North American roadrunner, which has recently been observed obeying stop signs and traffic lights, will understand 98 % of the highway code.

The 'Frisbee' was invented by the American Sioux Indian chief, Crazy Horse, who, after battle, would throw newly cut scalps at small Indian children.

In 1861, when Kansas became the 34th American State, President Abraham Lincoln demanded that the outline should match the shape of his head. The design was soon changed after his assassination in 1865.

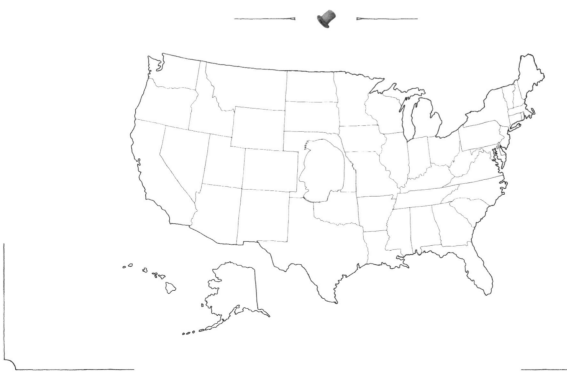

The first man-made object in space was not Sputnik 1, but a rocket made for a high school science project by thirteen-year-old Jimmy Jamas.

launched: Nevada Desert, 7:16am, 4th April, 1956 Pacific coast time

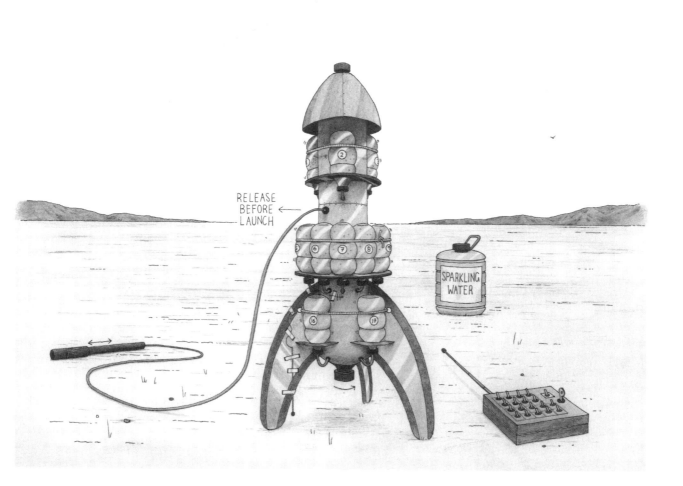

The G-forces on Coney Island's Cyclone roller coaster are so great, NASA used the ride to train astronauts for the early Apollo space missions.

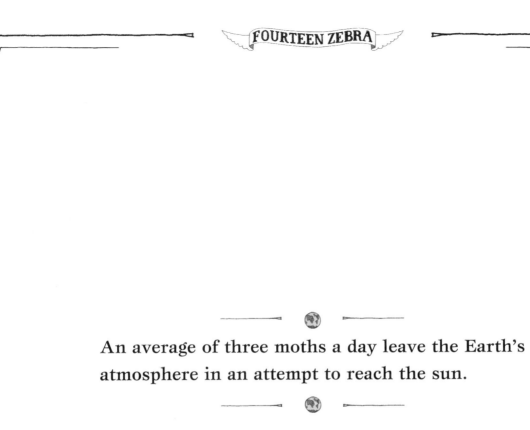

An average of three moths a day leave the Earth's atmosphere in an attempt to reach the sun.

Brain doctors are 70% more susceptible to headaches than doctors working in any other field. The Miami College of Medicine has a team of scientists dedicated to studying why this is.

FOURTEEN ZEBRA

IN 2001, DURING AN INDEPENDENT AUDIT AT NASA, IT
WAS DISCOVERED THAT FORMER SATELLITE TECHNICIAN,
BUDDY FAIRCHILD, WASTED OVER $200 BILLION LOOKING
AT HIMSELF FROM SPACE.

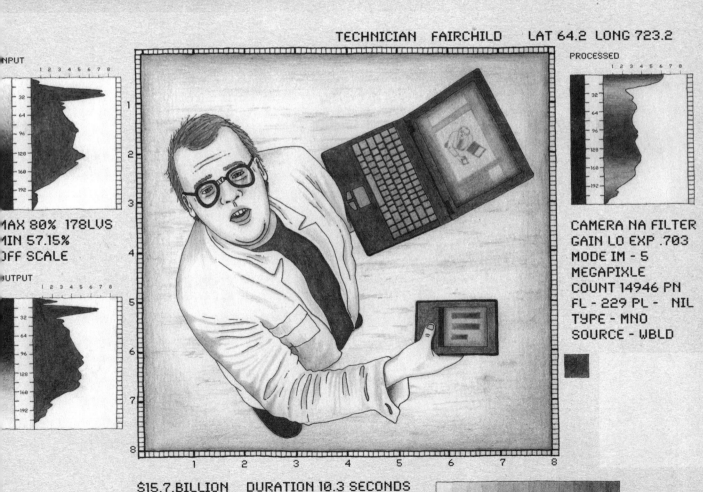

TECHNICIAN FAIRCHILD   LAT 64.2 LONG 723.2

INPUT

MAX 80% 178LVS
MIN 57.15%
OFF SCALE

OUTPUT

PROCESSED

CAMERA NA FILTER
GAIN LO EXP .703
MODE IM - 5
MEGAPIXLE
COUNT 14946 PN
FL - 229 PL - NIL
TYPE - MNO
SOURCE - WBLD

$15.7,BILLION   DURATION 10.3 SECONDS

FACT 73

STRETCH - AUTO ENDS-IN-L%-2.00 006
H - 2.00000 253L007 - 011 (HALF)

The largest ever balloon animal is a life-size replica of a woolly mammoth which can be seen at the Ohio Museum of Natural History.

WOOLLY MAMMOTH

The winner of the 1997 'Bird Spelling Bee' was a parrot named Chirpy who spelt the word *Salpiglossis* without even needing a further definition.

The 'trash trout' is a new species of fish recently discovered in the Everglades National Park which catches flies by mimicking litter.

In the same year as their famous first flight the Wright brothers also broke the world record for the furthest paper airplane throw.

Their paper airplane actually travelled further than their first powered flight.

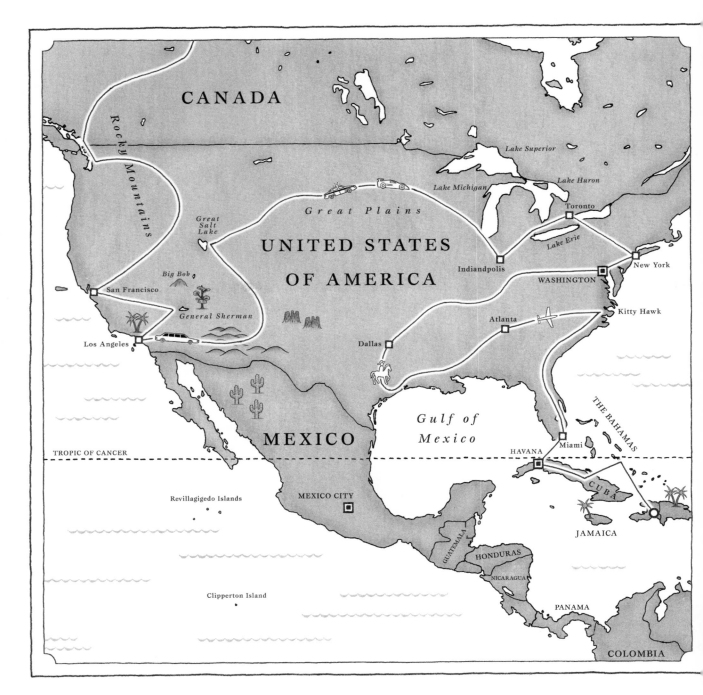

2nd October 2001 – Haiti

The hunt for the infamous Bolivian Yeti (last spotted in Haiti) continues. So far, it has been an arduous slog through the mountains and with no news yet of a genuine sighting, morale is low. Furthermore, Howlett is struggling to keep up after being shot in the leg with a tranquilizer dart. It was an unfortunate incident, but it was dark last night, and he should have told someone before going into the woods to bury his pencil shavings, especially as he has not washed or shaved for over three weeks.

We are close to defeat. Perhaps the lowest point so far was this morning, when we discovered the footprints we had been tracking for the past twelve days were in fact being made by our lead porter, José, who has unusually large feet.

The hunt continues…

The only multiple celled organism to reproduce asexually through cell division is the Guatemalan mountain gerbil. Mitosis occurs every three days.

The *ciparappouss fungiramus*, found deep in the heart of the Amazon rainforest, is the only plant to have a fully functioning brain. Botanists have determined that the plant has the same brain capacity as an eleven-year-old boy.

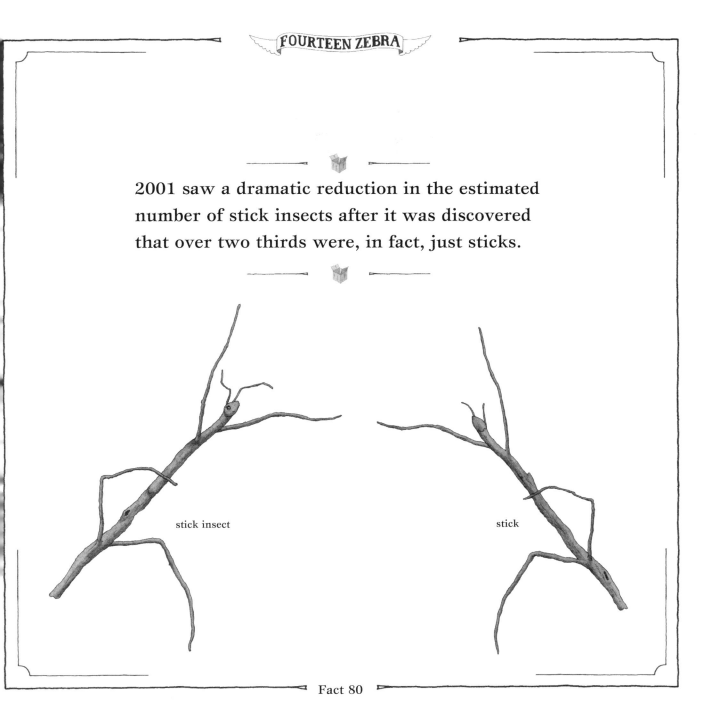

2001 saw a dramatic reduction in the estimated number of stick insects after it was discovered that over two thirds were, in fact, just sticks.

stick insect

stick

The Macca-Wanna tribe, found deep in the Amazon basin, are the only humans who have evolved to have eleven fingers: five on the left hand and six on the right. When hunting, this extra digit enables the tribesmen to harness more power in their bowstrings.

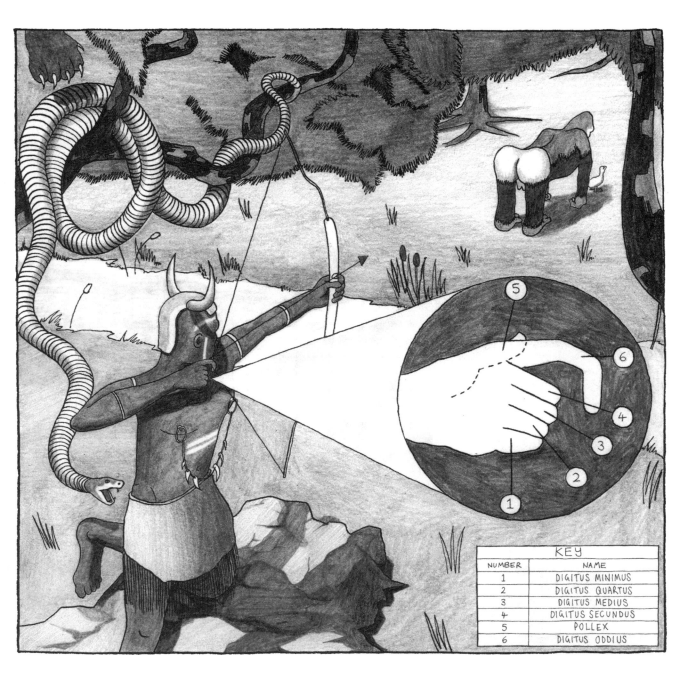

KEY	
NUMBER	NAME
1	DIGITUS MINIMUS
2	DIGITUS QUARTUS
3	DIGITUS MEDIUS
4	DIGITUS SECUNDUS
5	POLLEX
6	DIGITUS ODDIUS

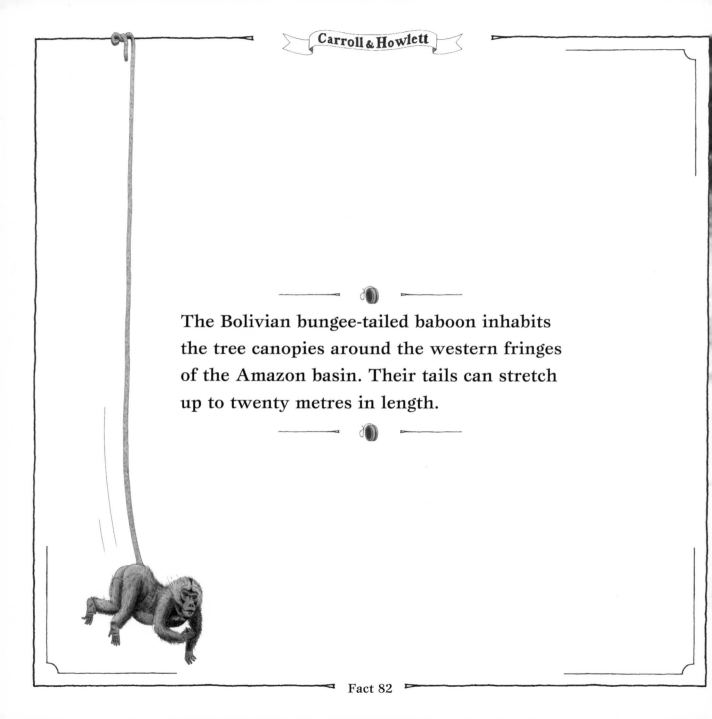

The Bolivian bungee-tailed baboon inhabits the tree canopies around the western fringes of the Amazon basin. Their tails can stretch up to twenty metres in length.

The Atacama sand slug is the only creature, other than the swan, which stays with one mate for their entire life. The slugs have a life span of approximately three days.

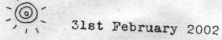

31st February 2002

Temperatures in this hazardous region of the
Atacama Desert can exceed 60°C. It is no wonder
travellers refer to it as 'the Mirage Mile'.
Extremely realistic hallucinations have been
reported in this area and already Howlett is
showing the first signs of delirium. In a
dehydrated frenzy, after I insisted we ration
the remaining sparkling water, he attacked me
with a modified pencil sharpener. He is
currently sitting on a nearby sand dune,
singing karaoke - badly.
I must admit, these mirages are very
convincing. After attempting a perfect
high-dive into what I believed to be an Olympic
sized swimming pool, I am now nursing a
severely cricked neck - I should have known.

Deep in the most remote waters of the South Pacific, in depths greater than 6000 metres, lives the rare popper fish, *dynamitus aquaticus*. When one of these giant fish dies it floats to the surface and explodes with the same force as a 1000lb bomb.

The greatest risk facing the future survival of the fanged-toothed ogre fish is that they are so ugly, they do not even want to mate with each other. In an attempt to change their visual appearance scientists are injecting them with swan DNA.

Charles Darwin loved the taste of dodo so much, he was both responsible for their discovery and extinction.

The Antarctic snow leopard will change the design of its spots every two years.

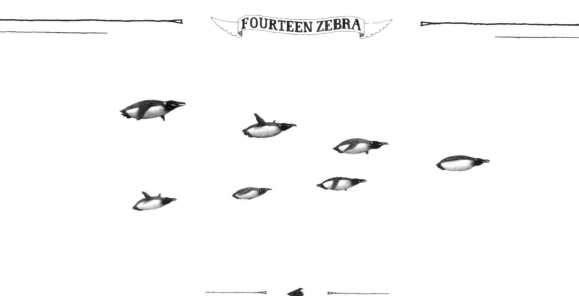

The yellow-eyed penguins which inhabit the craggy islands just off the coast of South America are the only variety of penguin able to fly.

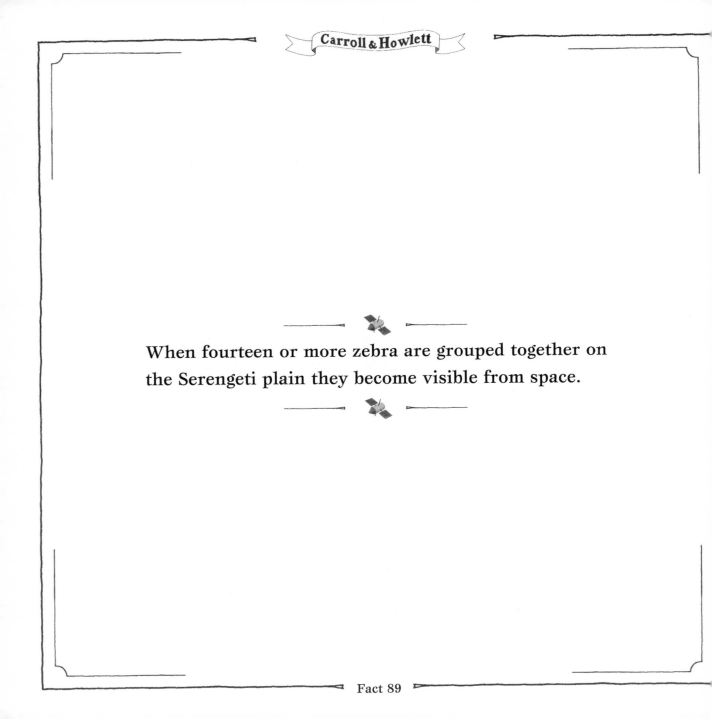

When fourteen or more zebra are grouped together on the Serengeti plain they become visible from space.

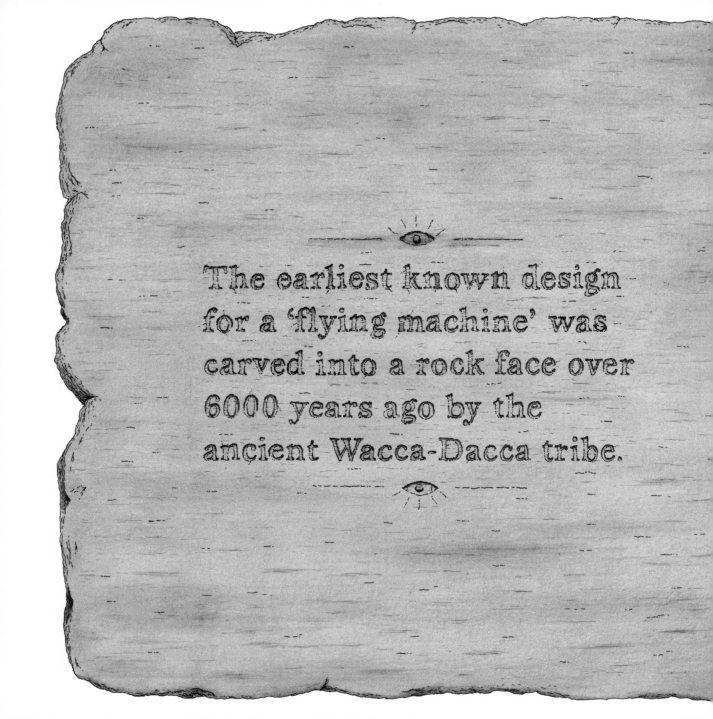

The earliest known design for a 'flying machine' was carved into a rock face over 6000 years ago by the ancient Wacca-Dacca tribe.

The 'pantomime horse' costume was devised by the Chacha-Coocoo people who inhabit the arid plains of Tanzania. After infiltrating an unsuspecting herd of antelope the tribesmen will jump out and attack.

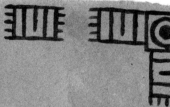

12th June 2002

We have lived among the Chacha-Coocoo people for some ten
weeks now and I am becoming concerned that Howlett is
trying too hard to integrate himself with the tribe.
Although it suits him, the seven-inch bone piercing through
his nose is perhaps one step too far, and he is now finding
it difficult to drink due to the large round disk implanted
into his bottom lip. Nonetheless, the African children have
enjoyed his art classes and seem to be grasping the basics
of abstract expressionism.

I have found it harder to gain the tribe's trust. I assumed
that dressing-up in a traditional two-man antelope costume
and joining the tribesmen on a hunt would win their favour.
Unfortunately, I found it almost impossible to tell the
difference between a real antelope and the disguised
tribesmen. The only thing I speared that afternoon was
chief Wannatootoo's thirteen-year-old son on the bottom.
I think we are beginning to outstay our welcome.

Nelson   Subject __Art Class__

SUBJECT REPORT

Marks					
B⁻	C⁺	D	C⁻	B⁻	C

e in amination	50/103
amination ark	12/20
chievement rade	C⁺

Nelson has made excellent progress this term and
I am pleased that he has recovered so quickly after
drinking the brown paint water! Sometimes, even I find
it difficult to distinguish between the paint water and
...he water from the village well. A Solid Start which must be
...ilt upon.

Signature __Nigel Howlett__

Subject __Art Class__

Marks					
B⁺	C⁻	A⁺	B⁻	B	A*

...hen Chief Wannatootoo
...for his complex redesign
...However, I disagree and
...to paint all the village
...red.

The combined mass of all the ants in the world is equal to that of Europa, one of the smaller moons orbiting Jupiter.

Colin, an agoraphobic giant silverback gorilla, is the only animal in history to have voluntarily left the wild and broken into a zoo. He currently resides at the Mombasa Zoological Park, and is free to leave whenever he wants.

One in every twenty-five Ethiopian children wear Prada T-shirts.

The first pair of sunglasses were designed by
the African tribal leader Chief Tabiboo who
fashioned frames using the bendy branches of
the Jubbalubba tree and stitched together
dried rat skins which helped to reduce glare.

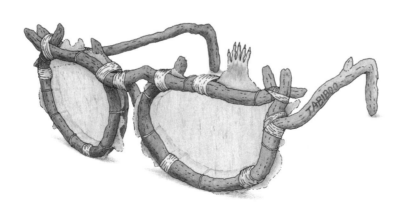

Over 90% of the world's wildlife has some kind of tag or tracking device fixed to their body.

Lightning strikes account for 42 % of all giraffe deaths.

There is more human blood in all the world's mosquitoes than in the entire population of the Gambia.

The avant-garde group of Moroccan artists known as the Casablancan Collective claim to have sculpted a new shape. It is rumoured to have more sides than a dodecahedron, half of which are curved.

UNVEILED
SUMMER 2008

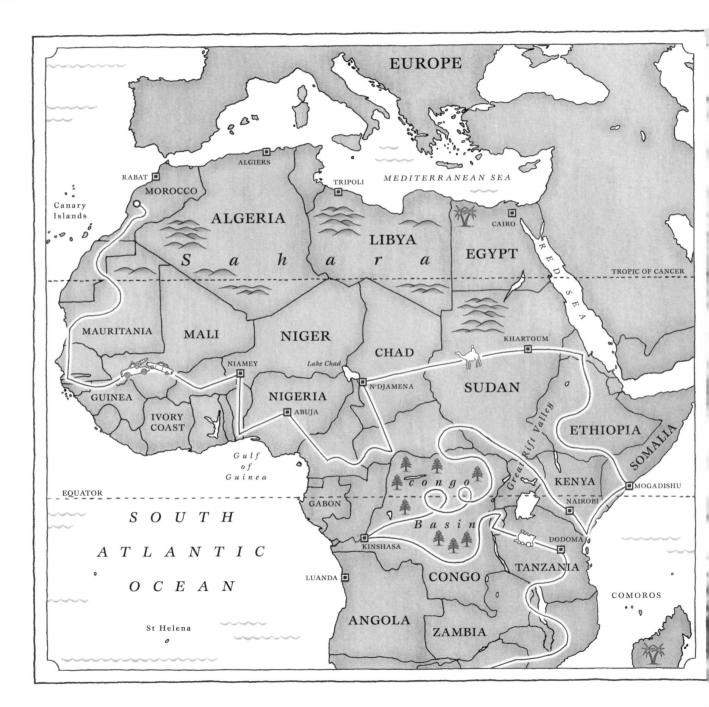

26th September 2002

Haggling is a risky business in Marrakech. Our
troubles started the moment Howlett casually tried on
a pair of rhino hide flip-flops and I looked
inquisitively at a gazelle skin sunhat. Suddenly, five
of the owner's sons, all wielding dangerous amounts of
mint tea, appeared from nowhere and surrounded us.
The only thing we had to offer in exchange for the
goods was a thorough medical examination by our
eleven-year-old expedition doctor, Bruno. They agreed,
but still required extra payment for the flip-flops.
I secured one flip-flop with a four-pack of half used
AA batteries and a Biro.
It was then that Howlett made a fatal error and
offered to draw the owner's family. Suitably impressed
by his portfolio, they agreed. However, Howlett was
unsure if he could fit all 148 members onto a single
A4 sheet, and it turned nasty. Backed into a corner,
and with no more batteries to exchange, we had no
choice but to let them keep Bruno.
Thankfully, the expedition will soon be over and he is
still far too young to be a practicing doctor in
England.

MUSTAFA'S World of LEATHERS

Thank you for shopping at

AUTH CODE 000001

Served by: MUSTAFA

RETAIN PLEASE THIS FOR YOUR RECORDS

QTY	CODE	M·W·L	CUSTOMER	GOODS VALUE
1	1	RHINO HIDE FLIP FLOP		
5	2		MEDICAL EXAMINATION	EQUAL
1	1	GAZELLE SKIN SUNHAT		
1	2		FOUR PACK AA BATTERIES AND BIRO	EQUAL
1	1	RHINO HIDE FLIP FLOP		
1	2		BRUNO THE DOCTOR	EQUAL

A pickpocket operating on the Ramblas in Barcelona will themselves be pickpocketed an average of three times per week.

In the 2002 budget, for the first time in sixty-eight years, the Chancellor of the Exchequer announced a 1p increase on the price of penny sweets.

The legendary 'Vera Valentine' is the only greyhound to have ever actually caught 'the hare' in a dog race.

Due to misprints in the first edition of the Oxford
English Dictionary, the spellings of the following
eleven words were inadvertently changed forever:

Awkward
Biscuit
Column
Flour
Knuckle
Juice
Neighbour
Reign
Scissors
Thorough
Tongue

Only 0.316% of Biro pens actually get used until they run out.

Found amongst the wreckage of the Titanic were the bodies of two polar bears which were thought to have become stranded on the iceberg as it floated down into the Atlantic.

17th November 2002

The sun has set and the White Cliffs have rolled
over the horizon into view - we are almost home.
After sixteen hours of uninterrupted cabaret
aboard the 'Disco Boat', Howlett has passed out
in the arms of a nineteen-year-old kissogram
from Southend-on-Sea.
As usual, I am left to hold the fraying tether
which encircles the neck of Gustav, who, as the
last surviving hairless mountain goat, is
destined for a fully customised,
climate-controlled pen at London Zoo.

The exact whereabouts of Carroll & Howlett is currently unknown. However, an undernourished carrier pigeon recently smashed through a window in the eastern wing of the Royal Society of Exploration with the following message clenched firmly in its beak:

At present we are somewhere in the desert tracking a pod of migrating Saharan sand whales, and would like to thank the following people all of whom have, in some form or another, offered us valuable help and advice:

Tom Davis, Dan Foley, Naomi Owen, Tom Veril Bryant, Peter Carroll, Sarah Langford, Muzi Quawson, Peter Wright, Christian Furr, Clare and Wensley Clarkson, Chief Wannatootoo and the Chacha-Coocoo tribe (good luck with the new album), everyone at the Royal Society of Exploration and John Blake Publishing. Finally, special thanks must be given to all the ladies at the pencil making factory in Delhi for their kind sponsorship and to Pete Finkle, the world's last surviving, and greatest, typewriter repairman (I am having problems typing the letter 'ɕ', please advise).

Carroll & Howlett, 2006